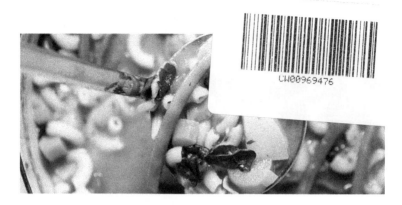

Soups and Fruit Dessert **Cookbook**

by Michelle Desire

Book 1:

SOUPS RECIPES FOR BEGINNER

Table of contents

ALMOND SOUP

(Serves 4)

Ingredients

- 225g/8oz blanched almonds minced.
- 3 egg yolks hard-boiled.
- 1.2 litres/2pt chicken stock.
- 25g/1oz butter softened.
- 25g/1oz plain flour.
- 125ml/4fl oz single cream.
- salt and freshly ground black pepper.

Procedure

1. Using a mortar and pestle, reduce the almonds to a paste with the egg yolks and 1 tablespoon of the stock. Set aside;

2. Make a beurre manié by working the butter and flour together into a smooth paste using a fork. Bring the remaining stock to a simmer in a heavy saucepan. Add the beurre manié in small knobs, whisking vigorously after each addition until completely dissolved. Whisk in the almond paste until smooth, then cook gently for 30 minutes;

3. Strain the soup through a sieve into a clean pan. Add the cream, and season with salt and pepper. Reheat gently and serve.

BOSTON BEAN SOUP

(Serves 4)

ingredients

- 850g/1¾lb canned cooked pinto beans, drained.
- 2 tomatoes, chopped.
- 1 celery stick, sliced.
- 1 medium onion, chopped.
- 1 bay leaf.
- 450ml/¾pt beef stock.
- salt and freshly ground black pepper.

Procedure

1. Put the beans, tomatoes, celery, onion, bay leaf and stock in a medium saucepan. Cover the pan, and bring the mixture to the boil over a medium-high heat;

2. Reduce the heat and simmer for about 20 minutes until the vegetables are quite soft. Leave the soup to sit, uncovered, for a further 20 minutes. Remove the bay leaf;

3. Pureé half the soup in a blender or food processor. Mix into the remainingsoup. Season to taste with salt and pepper, and serve.

CHICKEN NOODLE SOUP

(Serves 6)

ingredients

- 900ml/1½pt chicken stock.
- 1 bay leaf.
- 4 spring onions, sliced.
- 225g/8oz button mushrooms, sliced.
- 100g/4oz cooked skinless chicken breast, thinly sliced.
- 50g/2oz soup pasta such as orzo or ditalini.
- 150ml/5fl oz dry white wine.
- 1 tablespoon chopped fresh flat-leaf parsley.
- salt and ground black pepper.

Procedure

1. Put the stock and bay leaf into a heavy pan, and bring to the boil. Add the spring onions and mushrooms to the simmering stock;

2. Add the chicken to the soup, and season with salt and pepper. Heat through for 2-3 minutes;

3. Add the pasta, cover and simmer for 7-8 minutes;

4. Just before serving, add the wine and parsley, heat the soup through for 2-3 minutes, then check the seasoning and adjust if necessary. Serve hot.

CHICKEN SOUP

(serves 4)

ingredients

- 1 roast chicken carcass with meat left on.
- 225g/8oz chicken wings.
- 1 onion, diced.
- 1 leek, diced.
- 1 parsnip, diced.
- 6 whole black peppercorns.

Procedure

1. Preheat the oven to 150° C/300° F/ Gas mark 2. Put in a large heavy saucepan with the chicken wings;

2. Add the onion, leek and parsnip, and bring to the boil. While the water is heating, add the whole peppercorns;

3. Once the stock has boiled, transfer to an ovenproof dish and cook in the oven for 2 hours. Skim off any scum from the surface using a slotted spoon, and strain the stock you have created. Discard everything except for the chicken;

4. When cool enough to handle, take out the carcass and shred the chicken before returning it to the stock. Serve hot.

BORSCHT

(serves 4)

ingredients

- 900g/2lb large raw beetroot.
- 225g/8oz onion, diced.
- 225g/8oz leeks, sliced.
- 2 celery sticks, chopped.
- 50g/2oz butter.
- 600ml/1pt chicken stock.
- 1 bay leaf.
- 150ml/5fl oz soured cream.
- salt and freshly ground black pepper.

Procedure

1. Boil the beetroot whole in salted water for 15 minutes. Drain and refresh in cold water. Peel and cut into 2.5cm/1in chunks;

2. In a frying pan, gently sweat the onion, leek and celery in the butter until softened. Add the beetroot, stock and bay leaf. Bring to the boil, skim the surface, reduce the heat and simmer for 45 minutes;

3. Discard the bay leaf, and purée the soup in a blender or food processor. Return to a clean pan, season and bring back to the simmer. Remove from the heat, stir in the sour cream and serve.

BOSTON BEAN SOUP

(serves 4)

ingredients

- 850g/1¾lb canned cooked pinto beans, drained.
- 2 tomatoes, chopped.
- 1 celery stick, sliced.
- 1 medium onion, chopped.
- 1 bay leaf.
- 450ml/¾pt beef stock.
- salt and freshly ground black pepper.

Procedure

1. Put the beans, tomatoes, celery, onion, bay leaf and stock in a medium saucepan. Cover the pan, and bring the mixture to the boil over a medium-high heat;

2. Reduce the heat and simmer for about 20 minutes until the vegetables are quite soft. Leave the soup to sit, uncovered, for a further 20 minutes. Remove the bay leaf;

3. Pureé half the soup in a blender or food processor. Mix into the remaining soup. Season to taste with salt and pepper, and serve.

CARROT & CORIANDER SOUP

(Serves 6)

ingredients

- 175g/6oz onion, diced.
- 50g/2oz butter.
- 500g/1lb 2oz carrots, sliced.
- 1 garlic clove, finely chopped.
- 1.2 litres/2pt vegetable stock.
- 2 teaspoons caster sugar.
- 150ml/5fl oz whipping cream.
- 2 tablespoons chopped fresh coriander leaves.
- salt and freshly ground black pepper.

Procedure

1. In a heavy saucepan, gently sweat the onion in the butter until soft and translucent. Add the carrots to the pan, and cook, stirring from time to time, for a further 5 minutes;

2. Add the garlic and stock. Season with salt and pepper and the sugar. Bring to the boil, reduce the heat and simmer for 30 minutes;

3. Pour the contents of the pan into a blender or food processor, and blitz to a purée. Pour back into a clean pan, and add the cream and coriander. Taste and adjust the seasoning, then heat the soup through gently, stirring. Serve hot.

CATALAN SOUP

(Serves 6)

ingredients

- 1 tablespoon vegetable oil.
- 900g/2lb beef mince.
- 2 carrots, chopped.
- 2 onions, chopped.
- 2 tomatoes, chopped.
- 25g/1oz plain flour.
- 1.2 litres/2pt hot vegetable stock.

Procedure

1. Heat the oil in a flameproof casserole dish over a medium heat. Sauté the beef until it is just cooked, then remove and keep to one side. Sauté the carrots, onions and tomatoes in the same pan for a few minutes, stirring continuously to prevent sticking;

2. Blend in the flour using a wooden spoon, and cook for a few more minutes. Return the cooked mince to the casserole;

3. Cover the mixture with the hot stock, and simmer the soup gently for about 45 minutes. Serve hot.

CAULIFLOWER & WALNUT SOUP

(serves 4)

Ingredients

- 1 medium cauliflower, broken into florets.
- 1 onion, roughly chopped.
- 450ml/3/4pt vegetable stock.
- 450ml/3/4pt milk.
- 25g/1oz walnut pieces.
- salt and freshly ground black pepper.

Procedure

1. Put the cauliflower, onion and stock in a large heavy saucepan. Bring to the boil, cover and simmer for about 15 minutes until soft;

2. Add the milk and walnuts, and stir through. Purée in a blender or food processor until smooth;

3. Return the soup to the pan. Season to taste with salt and pepper, then bring to the boil - be careful not to scorch. Serve hot.

CELERY & STILTON SOUP

(serves 4)

Ingredients

- 4 celery sticks, finely chopped.
- 1 onion, finely chopped.
- 50g/2oz butter.
- 45g/1¹/₂oz plain flour.
- ¹/₂ glass white wine.
- 900ml/1¹/₂pt chicken stock.
- 300ml/10fl oz milk.
- 225g/8oz crumbled Stilton cheese.
- salt and freshly ground black pepper.

Procedure

1. In a heavy saucepan over a low heat, gently sweat the celery and onion in butter until soft. Add the flour and remove from the heat;

2. Pour in the wine and stock, stirring continuously. Return to the heat and slowly bring to the boil, stirring until the mixture thickens. Simmer for 25 minutes.

3. Add the milk, simmer for a further 2 minutes and remove from the heat. Whisk in the Stilton;

4. Purée the soup in a blender or food processor, then push through a sieve into a clean pan. Season with salt and pepper;

5. Reheat gently and serve.

CLAM CHOWDER

(serves 6)

Ingredients

- 8 celery sticks, chopped.
- 700g/1 1/2lb onions, chopped.
- 1.8kg/4lb red potatoes, diced.
- 900g/2lb canned clams with juice.
- 3 teaspoons dried thyme.
- 1 teaspoon dried oregano.
- 2 teaspoons dried basil.
- 225ml/8fl oz fish bouillon.
- 2 teaspoons ground white pepper.
- 225g/8oz butter.
- 250g/9oz plain flour.
- 3 garlic cloves, finely chopped.
- 1.2 litres/2pt milk.

Procedure

1. Put the celery, onions, potatoes, clams, thyme, oregano, basil, bouillon and pepper in a large heavy saucepan. Gently cook for 30-45 minutes until the vegetables and potatoes are soft;

2. To make a roux, melt the butter in a small heavy pan, add the flour and garlic, and stir constantly with a wooden spoon for a few minutes until slightly brown;

3. Combine the roux with the vegetable mixture and add the milk. Stir well and cook for 10 minutes. Serve hot.

COURGETTE & SPINACH SOUP

(serves 4)

Ingredients

- 2 tablespoons vegetable oil.
- 1 onion, chopped.
- 2 courgettes, chopped.
- 1 potato, chopped.
- 100g/4oz spinach, chopped.
- 3 sprigs of fresh flat-leaf parsley.
- 1.2 litres/2pt vegetable stock.
- 150ml/5fl oz double cream.
- salt and freshly ground black pepper.

Procedure

1. Heat the oil in a saucepan, and sweat the onion and courgette until the onion is transparent;

2. Add the potato, spinach, parsley and stock. Bring to the boil, reduce the heat and simmer the soup for 20 minutes. Allow to cool before blending or processing to a purée;

3. Return the soup to a clean pan, stir in the cream and season with salt and pepper. Reheat gently without boiling and serve.

HOT & SOUR SOUP

(serves 4-6)

Ingredients

- 8 dried shiitake mushrooms.
- 25g/1oz cornflour.
- 3 tablespoons dry sherry.
- 100g/4oz pork loin.
- 1.2 litres/2pt chicken stock.
- 50g/2oz bamboo shoots, sliced.
- 1 tablespoon light soy sauce.
- 2 tablespoons red wine vinegar.
- 1 egg, lightly beaten.
- 225g/8oz tofu, diced.
- salt and freshly ground black pepper.
- In a medium bowl, soak the mushrooms.

Procedure

1. In a medium bowl, soak the mushrooms in warm water for 20 minutes, then drain, squeeze out any excess moisture and cut into 1cm/1/2in slices;

2. In a small dish, stir the cornflour into the sherry and set aside;

3. Put the pork loin in a large heavy pan and completely cover with water. Simmer until tender, then cool and shred;

4. Bring the stock to the boil. Stir in the pork, mushrooms and bamboo shoots. Simmer for 10 minutes, then stir in the soy sauce and red wine vinegar. Season with salt and pepper, then stir in the reserved cornflour mixture. Keep stirring until the soup has thickened;

5. Remove from the heat and whisk in the egg. Mix in the tofu and heat through. Serve the soup hot.

FISH CHOWDER

(serves 10)

Ingredients

- 3 tablespoons olive oil.
- 200g/7oz onion, finely chopped.
- 200g/7oz celery, finely chopped.
- 150g/5oz carrot, finely chopped.
- 400g/14oz canned chopped tomatoes.
- 1 teaspoon finely chopped garlic.
- 100g/4oz plain flour.
- 1/2 teaspoon ground cinnamon.
- 1/2 teaspoon dried marjoram.
- 1/2 teaspoon dried oregano.
- 2.4 litres/4pt fish stock.
- 200g/7oz cooked boneless cod fillets, flaked.
- 25ml/1fl oz dark rum.

- 25ml/1fl oz Worcestershire sauce.
- 1 tablespoon Tabasco sauce.
- salt and ground black pepper.

Procedure

1. Heat the olive oil in a heavy saucepan over a medium heat. Sweat the vegetables, tomatoes and garlic for 5 minutes, stirring continuously;

2. Add the flour, cinnamon and herbs, and continue to cook for a further 2 minutes. Add the stock and bring to the boil, then crumble the fish into the pan with the rum, Worcestershire sauce and Tabasco. Simmer for 1 hour, stirring occasionally;

3. Season with salt and pepper, and serve hot.

FRENCH BEAN SOUP

(serves 4)

Ingredients

- 1 tablespoon olive oil.
- 1 onion, chopped.
- 2 celery sticks, thinly sliced.
- 3 garlic cloves, minced.
- 550g/1lb 4oz canned cooked cannellini beans, drained.
- 400ml/14fl oz vegetable stock.
- 125ml/4fl oz white wine.
- 3 sprigs of fresh rosemary.
- 1/4 teaspoon ground white pepper.
- 100g/4oz mozzarella cheese, grated.

Procedure

1. Heat the oil in a large saucepan over a medium-high heat. Add the onion, celery and garlic, and sweat for 5 minutes until soft, stirring frequently;

2. Add the remaining ingredients except the cheese, and bring the mixture to the boil. Reduce the heat and cover the pan, then simmer for 10–15 minutes;

3. To serve, remove and discard the rosemary sprigs. Ladle the soup into warm bowls, and top each serving with a little of the cheese.

GAZPACHO

(serves 6)

Ingredients

- 2 large garlic cloves.
- 1 egg yolk.
- 1 thick slice bread, crust removed.
- 90ml/3fl oz olive oil.
- 450g/1lb canned whole peeled plum tomatoes.
- 900g/2lb ripe tomatoes, deseeded and chopped.
- 1 large onion, chopped.
- 1 cucumber, peeled and chopped.
- 2 red peppers, seeded and chopped.
- 1 tablespoon tomato purée sea.
- salt and freshly ground black pepper.
- 2 lemons, cut into wedges, to serve.

Procedure

1. Put the garlic, egg yolk and bread in a blender or food processor. With the motor running, slowly add the oil in a thin steady stream until the mixture turns to mayonnaise;

2. Add the chopped tomatoes, onion, cucumber, peppers and tomato purée in batches, and continue blending until smooth;

3. Season with salt and pepper to taste, and chill in the refrigerator until ready to serve;

4. Just before serving, check the seasoning and adjust if necessary. Serve cold with lemon wedges for squeezing over.

FRENCH ONION SOUP

(serves 6)

Ingredients

- 900g/2lb onions, thinly sliced.
- 50g/2oz butter.
- 900ml/11/2pt vegetable stock.
- salt and freshly ground black pepper.

Procedure

1. Fry the onions very gently in the butter in a covered saucepan for 15 minutes until soft and starting to caramelize. Remove the lid, increase the heat and fry, stirring, for about 20 minutes until the onions are a rich golden brown;

2. Add the stock and bring to the boil. Reduce the heat, part-cover and simmer for 15 minutes. Season with salt and pepper, and serve.

CHILLED CUCUMBER SOUP

(serves 6-8)

Ingredients

- 1 onion, diced 50g/2oz butter.
- 550g/1lb 4oz cucumber, diced.
- 1.8 litres/3pt vegetable stock.
- 2 tablespoons chopped fresh parsley.
- juice of 1/2 lemon.
- 600ml/1pt single cream.
- salt and freshly ground black pepper.

Procedure

1. In a heavy saucepan, gently sweat the onion in the butter until soft and translucent, but not coloured. Add the cucumber and continue to cook gently for a further 5 minutes;

2. Pour in the stock and bring to the boil. Reduce the heat, season with salt and pepper, and simmer for 5 minutes. Add the parsley and lemon juice, and continue to cook for a further 5 minutes;

3. Blend or process the soup to a purée. Allow to cool, then transfer to the refrigerator to chill;

4. When ready to serve, whisk in the single cream. Serve chilled.

BEEF & LENTIL SOUP

(serves 8)

Ingredients

- 300g/11oz dried red lentils, picked and rinsed.
- 225g/8oz stewing beef, cubed.
- 1 leek, finely chopped.
- 3 large carrots, finely chopped.
- 2 celery sticks, finely chopped.
- 1 tablespoon vegetable oil.
- 2 onions, finely chopped.
- 2 tablespoons plain flour.
- 50ml/2fl oz dry white wine.

Procedure

1. Bring 1.8 litres/3pt water to the boil in a large heavy saucepan. Add the lentils, beef, leek, carrots and celery. Return to the boil, then reduce the heat, cover the pan and simmer for 40 minutes;

2. Remove the beef, drain on kitchen paper and brown in the oil in a frying pan over a high heat. When the pan is very hot, add the onions and sauté for 15 minutes, stirring frequently. Sprinkle the flour over the onions and stir with a wooden spoon until the flour browns;

3. Pour 225ml/8fl oz of the lentil mixture over the onions and stir vigorously. Add the white wine; cook for a further 1 minute. Tip the contents of the frying pan into the lentil mixture. Simmer for 30 minutes before serving.

LEEK & POTATO SOUP

(serves 4)

Ingredients

- 50g/2oz butter.
- 450g/1lb leeks, trimmed and finely sliced.
- 700g/11/2lb potatoes, roughly chopped.
- 900ml/11/2pt vegetable stock.
- 4 sprigs of fresh rosemary.
- 450ml/3/4pt milk.
- 2 tablespoons chopped fresh flat-leaf parsley.
- 2 tablespoons crème fraiche.
- salt and ground black pepper.

Procedure

1. Melt the butter in a large saucepan, add the leeks and sweat gently for 5 minutes, stirring frequently. Add the potatoes, stock, rosemary and milk. Bring to the boil, then reduce the heat, cover and simmer gently for 20–25 minutes until the vegetables are tender. Remove from the heat;

2. Cool for 10 minutes. Discard the rosemary, then pour into a blender or food processor, and purée until smooth. Return to a clean pan, and stir in the parsley and crème fraîche. Season to taste. Reheat gently and serve.

LETTUCE SOUP

(serves 6)

Ingredients

- 600ml/1pt chicken stock.
- 1 round lettuce, shredded.
- 1 small onion, chopped.
- 25g/1oz butter.
- 1/2 teaspoon freshly grated nutmeg.
- 300ml/10fl oz milk.
- 1 egg yolk.
- 2 tablespoons single cream.
- salt and freshly ground black pepper.

Procedure

1. Bring the stock to the boil, add the lettuce and boil for 5 minutes. In a separate pan, sweat the onion in the butter for 3 minutes until soft;

2. Pour in the lettuce and stock, and season with the nutmeg, salt and pepper. Simmer for 5 minutes until the onion is very soft. Purée in a blender or food processor, and return to the saucepan. Stir in the milk;

3. Whisk the egg yolk and cream together. Whisk in a little of the soup, then pour back into the remaining soup and heat through, stirring all the while. Do not allow to boil or the egg will curdle. Serve hot.

LOBSTER BISQUE

(serves 4)

Ingredients

- 700g/11/2lb lobster.
- 100g/4oz butter.
- 50g/2oz carrots, diced.
- 1 small onion, chopped.
- 1/2 bay leaf.
- pinch of thyme.
- 2 sprigs of fresh flat-leaf parsley.
- 3 tablespoons Cognac.
- 75ml/3fl oz dry white wine.
- 125ml/4fl oz fish stock.
- 50g/2oz plain flour.
- 350ml/12fl oz boiling milk.
- 3 tablespoons double cream.
- salt and freshly ground black pepper.

Procedure

1. Crack the lobster claws and cut the body and tail into four or five pieces. Set aside;

2. Sauté the carrots and onion in 25g/1oz of the butter for 5 minutes. Add the bay leaf, thyme, parsley and lobster, and cook for about 5 minutes until the lobster turns red. Add 2 tablespoons of the Cognac and ignite;

3. When the flames die down, add the wine and stock, and simmer for 20 minutes;

4. Remove the meat from the lobster, reserving the shells and broth;

5. Melt the remaining butter in a saucepan. Add the flour and cook, stirring constantly, for 2 minutes to make a roux. Gradually add the boiling milk, whisking or stirring with a wooden spoon until smooth;

6. Crush the lobster shells and add to the sauce. Add the reserved broth with the vegetables and simmer, covered, for 1 hour. Strain through a sieve into a clean pan. Bring to the boil and stir in the cream;

7. To serve, add the lobster meat and the remaining Cognac. Season with salt and pepper, and serve hot.

MUSHROOM SOUP

(serves 4)

Ingredients

- 350g/12oz mushrooms, finely chopped.
- 50g/2oz butter.
- 3 tablespoons chopped fresh flat-leaf parsley.
- 2 tablespoons fresh breadcrumbs (without any crust).
- 1/2 garlic clove.
- 900ml /11/2 pt chicken stock.
- pinch of freshly grated nutmeg.
- 2 tablespoons double cream.
- salt and ground black pepper.

Procedure

1. Sauté the mushroom with the butter in a heavy saucepan for a few minutes. Add the parsley and cook, stirring, until soft;

2. Add the breadcrumbs and garlic, stir and pour in the chicken stock with a pinch of nutmeg. Season with salt and pepper. Bring to the boil and simmer for 15 minutes;

3. Purée the soup in a food processor or blender until smooth. Return to a clean pan, stir in the cream and reheat gently. Serve hot.

MINESTRONE

(serves 4-6)

Ingredients

- 100g/4oz carrot, chopped.
- 100g/4oz celery, chopped.
- 100g/4oz onion, chopped.
- 2 garlic cloves, minced.
- 1 tablespoon chopped fresh basil.
- 1 tablespoon chopped fresh oregano.
- 1/2 teaspoon ground pepper.
- 425g/15oz canned cooked red kidney beans, drained.
- 400g/14oz canned chopped tomatoes.
- 150g/5oz cabbage, coarsely chopped.
- 1 courgette, chopped.
- 75g/3oz soup pasta such as orzo or ditalini.

Procedure

1. Pour 900ml/11/2pt water into a large heavy saucepan. Add the carrot, celery, onion, garlic, basil, oregano and pepper;

2. Bring to the boil, then reduce the heat. Cover the pan, and simmer the mixture for 15 minutes;

3. Add the kidney beans to the pan with the tomatoes, cabbage, courgette and pasta. Return to the boil and reduce the heat. Cover the pan and simmer for 5– 10 minutes until the pasta is cooked until al dente. Serve hot.

MULLIGATAWNY

(serves 12)

Ingredients

- 1 garlic clove, minced.
- 1/4 teaspoon ground cumin.
- 6 cloves, finely crushed.
- 1 tablespoon curry powder.
- 1/4 teaspoon ground ginger.
- 50g/2oz butter.
- 1 roasting chicken, cut into serving pieces.
- 3 celery sticks, thinly sliced.
- 2 large onions, chopped.
- 2 carrots, diced.
- 1 leek, white part only, thinly sliced.

- litres/4pt chicken stock.
- salt and freshly ground black pepper.
- 200g/7oz long-grain rice.
- 2 dessert apples, peeled, cored and diced.
- 225ml/8fl oz plain yogurt.
- 2 tablespoons lemon juice.
- 150ml/5fl oz whipping cream, gently warmed.

Procedure

1. Combine the garlic and spices. Melt the butter in a large heavy frying pan over a medium-high heat. Add the chicken and sauté until lightly browned on all sides. Transfer the chicken to a casserole dish;

2. Drain all but 1 tablespoon of the fat from the frying pan. Add the celery, onion, carrot, leek and spice mixture, and blend well until the spices are aromatic. Add a small ladle of stock and cook over a low heat, stirring constantly, until the vegetables are tender. Add to the chicken;

3. Stir the remaining stock into the casserole dish, and season with salt and pepper. Cover and simmer for 30 minutes;

4. Remove the chicken with a slotted spoon and set aside. Add the rice to the soup and continue cooking for a further 15 minutes;

5. When the chicken is cool enough to handle, cut into bite-sized pieces, discarding the skin and bones. Return the chicken to the soup. Peel, core and discarding the skin and bones. Return the chicken to the soup. Peel, core and dice the apples, and blend into the soup with the yogurt. Simmer for 10 minutes;

6. Stir in the lemon juice, then blend in the cream. Taste and adjust the seasoning if necessary. Serve hot.

OXTAIL SOUP

(serves 2)

Ingredients

- 25g/1oz beef dripping.
- 2 oxtails.
- 1 large onion, diced.
- 1 carrot, diced.
- 2 celery sticks.
- 2 sprigs of fresh flat-leaf parsley.
- 1 bay leaf.
- 2 tablespoons pearl barley.
- 1 tablespoon plain flour mixed with 2 tablespoons water.
- salt and freshly ground black pepper.

Procedure

1. Melt the dripping in a heavy saucepan. Fry the oxtails, onion and carrot until brown, then add 1.2 litres/2pt water;

2. Tie the celery, parsley and bay leaf together, and add to the soup;

3. Bring to the boil, add the pearl barley and simmer for 4 hours, skimming off any scum that rises to the surface;

4. Remove the large bones and celery, parsley and bay leaf, then thicken the soup with the flour paste, stirring all the while;

5. Season with salt and pepper, and serve hot.

OYSTER SOUP

(serves 4)

Ingredients

- 50g/2oz butter.
- 50g/2oz plain flour.
- 900ml/11/2pt fish stock.
- 12 large oysters, shucked and quartered.
- 2 tablespoons finely chopped fresh flat-leaf parsley.
- 1 lemon, cut into wedges, to serve.

Procedure

1. Heat the butter and, using a wooden spoon, stir in the flour and cook for 2 minutes. Stir in the stock slowly, until smooth and thick;

2. Put the oysters in the stock and simmer for no more than 3 minutes;

3. Sprinkle the soup with the parsley and serve with lemon wedges.

CHILLED PEA SOUP

(serves 5)

Ingredients

- large fennel bulb, coarsely chopped.
- 275g/10oz frozen peas, thawed.
- 75ml/3fl oz double cream.
- 1 teaspoon lemon liqueur such as lemon schnapps or limoncello.
- 1 teaspoon chopped spring onion.
- salt and freshly ground black pepper.
- 1 tablespoon chopped fresh mint, to garnish.

Procedure

1. Put the fennel and 1.2 litres/2pt water in a large pan over a medium-high heat, and simmer for 10 minutes. Strain the fennel broth and discard the solids;

2. Purée the peas, cream, liqueur and spring onions in a blender or food processor;

3. Season with salt and pepper, then add the broth and blend until smooth;

4. Strain the soup through a sieve into a metal bowl. Set in a larger bowl, and fill the outer bowl with iced water to reach halfway up side of the inner bowl. Stir until the soup is cold. Serve garnished with mint.

PEA & MINT SOUP

(serves 6)

Ingredients

- 450g/1lb frozen peas.
- 900ml/11/2pt vegetable stock.
- pinch of granulated sugar.
- 1 large sprig of fresh mint.
- 1 egg yolk.
- 50ml/2fl oz single cream.
- salt and freshly ground black pepper.

Procedure

1. Put the peas in a large pan with the stock, sugar, mint and a little salt and pepper. Bring to the boil, reduce the heat, cover and simmer for 15 minutes;

2. Discard the mint, then purée the mixture in a blender or food processor. Return to the heat;

3. Blend the egg yolk with half the cream and stir into the soup. Return the soup to a clean pan and reheat, but do not allow to boil;

4. Taste and adjust the seasoning if necessary. Serve garnished with the remaining cream.

POTATO SOUP

(serves 6)

Ingredients

- 8 rashers back bacon.
- 200g/7oz onion, chopped.
- 450g/1lb potatoes, cubed.
- 275g/10oz canned condensed chicken soup.
- 600ml/1pt milk.
- 1 teaspoon dried dill.
- salt and freshly ground black pepper.

Procedure

1. In a large saucepan, sauté the bacon until crisp. Remove and drain on kitchen paper. Sauté the onions in the bacon fat over a medium heat until soft and golden;

2. Add the potatoes and enough water to cover. Cover the pan, and cook for 15–20 minutes until the potatoes are tender;

3. Stir together the condensed soup and milk until smooth, and add to potato mixture. Heat but do not allow to boil. Season with salt and pepper to taste, and stir in the dill;

4. Crumble the bacon and sprinkle on top to garnish. Serve hot.

PUMPKIN SOUP

(serves 4)

Ingredients

- 900ml/1 1/2pt milk.
- 500g/1lb 2oz pumpkin, peeled, deseeded and cubed.
- 1 teaspoon ground nutmeg.
- 300ml/10fl oz single cream.
- salt and freshly ground black pepper.
- extra virgin olive oil for drizzling.

Procedure

- Put milk and pumpkin in a heavy saucepan. Add the nutmeg, and season with salt and pepper. Bring to the boil. Reduce the heat and simmer until the pumpkin is tender;
- Using a food processor or hand-held blender, purée until smooth;
- Return to a clean pan, and stir in the cream. Check the seasoning and adjust if necessary, then gently reheat the soup;
- Serve hot, garnished with a drizzle of extra virgin olive oil.

RED PEPPER SOUP

(serves 6)

Ingredients

- 4 red peppers.
- 4 tomatoes.
- 50ml/2fl oz vegetable oil.
- 1/2 teaspoon dried marjoram.
- 1/2 teaspoon dried mixed herbs.
- 2 garlic cloves, crushed.
- 1 teaspoon mild curry paste.
- 1 red onion, sliced.
- 1 leek, white part only, sliced.
- 1 teaspoon sweet chilli sauce.
- salt and freshly ground black pepper.

Procedure

1. Cut the peppers into quarters. Remove the seeds and membrane. Grill until the skin blackens and blisters. Place on a cutting board, cover with a tea towel and allow to cool before removing and discarding the skin;

2. Mark a small cross on the top of each tomato. Put in a bowl and cover with boiling water for about 2 minutes. Drain and cool. Skin, halve and remove the seeds;

3. Heat the oil in a large heavy pan over a low heat, and add the marjoram, mixed herbs, garlic and curry paste. Stir for 1 minute until aromatic, then add the onion and leek. Cook for a further 3 minutes. Add the cabbage, tomatoes, peppers and 1.2 litres/2pt water. Bring to the boil, reduce the heat and simmer for 20 minutes;

4. Allow the soup to cool slightly, then purée in a blender or food processor for 30 seconds or until smooth. Return to the pan and reheat gently. Stir in the chilli sauce, and season with salt and pepper. Serve hot.

SCOTCH BROTH

(serves 6-8)

Ingredients

- 900g/2lb neck of lamb, cubed.
- 1 large onion, chopped.
- 50g/2oz pearl barley.
- 1 bouquet garni.
- 1 large carrot, chopped.
- 1 turnip, chopped.
- 3 leeks, chopped.
- 1/2 small white cabbage, shredded.
- salt and freshly ground black pepper.

Procedure

1. Put the lamb and 1.8 litres/3pt water in a large heavy saucepan, and bring to the boil. Skim off any scum from the surface, then stir in the onion, pearl barley and bouquet garni. Bring the soup back to the boil, part-cover the pan and simmer gently for 1 hour;

2. Add the remaining vegetables, and season with salt and pepper. Bring to the boil again, part-cover and simmer for 35 minutes;

3. Use kitchen paper to skim surplus fat from the top of the soup. Discard the bouquet garni and serve hot.

TOMATO SOUP

(serves 6)

Ingredients

- 25g/1oz butter.
- 1 large onion, sliced.
- 1 garlic clove, crushed.
- 2 rashers rindless streaky bacon, chopped.
- 700g/11/2lb tomatoes, peeled and chopped.
- 1 tablespoon chopped fresh flat-leaf parsley.
- 1/2 teaspoon chopped fresh thyme.
- 1/2 teaspoon grated lemon zest.
- 1 teaspoon soft brown sugar.
- 900ml/11/2pt vegetable stock.
- 1 tablespoon double cream.
- salt and freshly ground black pepper.
- 1 tablespoon chopped fresh chives, to serve.

Procedure

1. Heat the butter in a heavy pan. Sweat the onion for a few minutes until soft. Add the garlic and bacon. Fry for 2 minutes without browning the bacon. Add the tomatoes and fry for a further 2 minutes. Add the other ingredients except the cream and chives. Cook, covered, for 25 minutes;

2. Blend or process the soup into a purée, and adjust the seasoning if necessary. Add a dollop of cream and the chives to each bowl to serve.

VEGETABLE SOUP

(serves 6)

Ingredients

- 1 onion, diced.
- 3 garlic cloves, finely chopped.
- 1 tablespoon olive oil.
- 175g/6oz carrots, chopped.
- 175g/6oz celery, chopped.
- 1 small courgette, chopped.
- 1 small yellow squash, chopped.
- 200g/7oz fresh broccoli, broken into florets.
- 200g/7oz fresh cauliflower, chopped.
- 100g/4oz mushrooms, sliced.
- 400g/14oz canned chopped tomatoes.

- 200ml/7fl oz tomato sauce.
- 1 teaspoon dried basil.
- 1 teaspoon dried oregano.
- 3 chicken stock cubes, crumbled.

Procedure

1. Lightly sauté the garlic and onions in the oil. Add the carrots and celery, and sweat for 3-5 minutes;

2. Add the courgette and squash. Cook for a further 3-5 minutes, then add the remaining ingredients and 1.8 litres/3pt water. Bring to the boil and simmer for 15 minutes. Serve hot.

VEGETABLE MINESTRONE

(serves 6)

Ingredients

- pinch of saffron strands.
- 1 onion, chopped.
- 1 leek, sliced.
- 1 celery stick, sliced.
- 2 carrots, diced.
- 3 garlic cloves, crushed.
- 600ml/1pt chicken stock.
- 850g/13/4lb canned chopped tomatoes.
- 50g/2oz frozen peas.
- 50g/2oz soup pasta.
- 1 teaspoon caster sugar.
- salt and freshly ground black pepper.

Procedure

1. Soak the saffron strands in 1 tablespoon boiling water. Leave to stand for 10 minutes;
2. Put the onion, leek, celery, carrots and garlic in a large pan. Add the stock, bring to the boil, cover and simmer for about 10 minutes;
3. Add the tomatoes, the saffron and its soaking liquid and the peas. Bring back to the boil and add the pasta. Simmer for 10 minutes until the pasta is al dente;
4. Sprinkle in the sugar, and season with salt and pepper. Stir through and serve hot.

VICHYSSOISE

(serves 6)

Ingredients

- 50g/2oz butter.
- 3 large leeks, trimmed and thinly sliced.
- 1 onion, thinly sliced.
- 500g/1lb 2oz potatoes, chopped).
- 900ml/11/2pt vegetable stock.
- 2 teaspoons lemon juice.
- pinch of ground nutmeg.
- 1/4 teaspoon ground coriander.
- 1 bay leaf.
- 1 egg yolk.
- 150ml/5fl oz single cream.
- salt and freshly ground black pepper.

Procedure

1. Melt the butter in a saucepan, and sweat the leeks and onion, stirring occasionally, for about 5 minutes. Add the potatoes, stock, lemon juice, nutmeg, coriander and bay leaf. Season with salt and pepper. Bring to the boil, cover and simmer for 30 minutes until the vegetables are soft;

2. Cool the soup a little, remove the bay leaf and purée the soup in a blender or food processor until smooth. Pour into a clean pan;

3. Blend the egg yolk into the cream, add a little of the soup to the mixture, then whisk it all back into the soup and reheat gently. Cool and chill before serving.

WATERCRESS SOUP

(serves 6)

Ingredients

- 1 onion, chopped.
- 15g/1/2oz butter.
- 350g/12oz watercress, roughly chopped.
- 1 tablespoon plain flour.
- 1.2 litres/2pt vegetable stock.
- 1/4 teaspoon grated nutmeg.
- 50ml/2fl oz single cream.
- 2 eggs, hard-boiled and finely chopped.
- salt and freshly ground black pepper.

Procedure

1. Sweat the onion in the butter for 2 minutes, add the watercress and cook, stirring with a wooden spoon, for a further 2 minutes. Stir in the flour. Remove from the heat and gradually blend in the stock;

2. Return to the heat, and bring to the boil, stirring. Season with salt, pepper and nutmeg. Reduce the heat and simmer for 20 minutes;

3. Blend or process to a purée, and return to a clean pan. Stir in the cream and reheat gently. Sprinkle the chopped eggs on top and serve.

CONSOMMÉ

(serves 6)

Ingredients

- 1.25 litres/2¼pt beef stock.
- 225g/8oz extra lean beef mince.
- 2 tomatoes, chopped.
- 2 large carrots, chopped.
- 1 large onion, chopped.
- 2 celery sticks, chopped.
- 1 turnip, chopped.
- 1 bouquet garni.
- 2 egg whites.
- shells of 2 eggs, crushed.
- 1 tablespoon sherry.
- salt and freshly ground black pepper.

Procedure

1. Put the stock and beef mince in a heavy saucepan. Add the tomatoes, carrots, onion, celery, turnip, bouquet garni, egg whites, egg shells and plenty of seasoning;
2. Bring almost to the boiling point, whisking all the time with a flat whisk;
3. Cover and simmer for 1 hour, taking care not to allow the layer of froth on top of the soup to break;
4. Carefully pour the soup through a scalded fine cloth such as muslin, keeping the froth back. Repeat if necessary until the liquid is clear. Add the sherry and reheat. Serve hot.

ONION AVGOLEMONO SOUP

(serves 6)

Ingredients

- 4 large onions, thinly sliced.
- 50g/2oz low-fat spread or butter.
- 450ml/3/4pt vegetable stock.
- 450ml/3/4pt skimmed milk.
- 2 egg yolks.
- 1/2 teaspoon freshly squeezed lemon juice.
- 2 thick slices wholemeal bread, cubed.
- salt and freshly ground black pepper.

Procedure

1. Preheat the oven to 200° C/400° F/Gas mark 6;

2. Melt the low-fat spread or butter in a heavy saucepan, add the onions and cook gently, covered, for 10 minutes, stirring from time to time, until soft. Add the stock, and season with a little salt and pepper. Bring to the boil, reduce the heat and simmer gently for 30 minutes;

3. Stir in the milk and heat through;

4. Whisk the egg yolks with the lemon juice. Add 2 ladlefuls of the hot soup and whisk well. Stir the egg and lemon mixture into the soup, and heat through gently, still stirring, until slightly thickened. Do not allow the soup to boil or the egg will curdle;

5. To make the croûtons, spread out the bread cubes on a baking tray, and bake in the oven for 10 minutes until a deep golden brown;

6. Ladle the soup into warm individual bowls, and sprinkle with the croûtons just before serving.

CHINESE CABBAGE SOUP

(serves 4)

Ingredients

- 450g/1lb pak choi.
- 600ml/1pt vegetable stock.
- 1 tablespoon rice wine vinegar.
- 1 tablespoon light soy sauce.
- 1 tablespoon caster sugar.
- 1 tablespoon dry sherry.
- 1 fresh red chilli, seeded and thinly sliced.
- 1 tablespoon cornflour.

Procedure

1. Wash the pak choi thoroughly under cold running water, rinse and drain. Pat dry with kitchen paper. Trim the stems from the pak choi, and shred the leaves;

2. Heat the stock in a large heavy saucepan. Add the pak choi and cook for 10–15 minutes;

3. Mix together the vinegar, soy sauce, sugar and sherry in a small bowl. Add this mixture to the stock, together with the chilli. Bring to the boil, reduce the heat and cook for 2–3 minutes;

4. Blend the cornflour with 2 tablespoons water to form a paste, and gradually stir into the soup. Cook, stirring constantly, until it thickens. Cook for a further 4–5 minutes, then ladle the soup into warm individual serving bowls and serve immediately.

RED ONION & BEETROOT SOUP

(serves 6)

Ingredients

- 2 teaspoons olive oil.
- 350g/12oz red onions, sliced.
- 2 garlic cloves, crushed.
- 275g/10oz cooked beetroot, cut into matchsticks.
- 1.2 litres/2pt vegetable stock.
- 50g/2oz soup pasta, cooked until al dente.
- 2 tablespoons raspberry vinegar.
- salt and freshly ground black pepper.

Procedure

1. Heat the oil in a casserole dish over a low heat, and add the onion and garlic. Sweat gently for 20 minutes or until soft and tender;

2. Add the beetroot, stock, pasta and vinegar, and heat through. Season with salt and pepper to taste, and serve hot.

SMOOTH CHEESE SOUP

(serves 4)

Ingredients

- 1 large potato, diced.
- 1 large carrot, diced.
- 1 small onion, diced.
- 1 celery stick, diced.
- 600ml/1pt vegetable stock.
- 1/2 teaspoon dried mixed herbs.
- 100g/4oz low-fat Cheddar cheese, grated.
- 150ml/5fl oz skimmed milk.

Procedure

1. Put the vegetables in a saucepan with the stock and herbs. Bring to the boil, reduce the heat, part-cover and simmer gently for 15 minutes until the vegetables are soft;

2. Purée in a blender or food processor, and return to the pan. Add the cheese and milk, and heat gently until the cheese melts. Ladle into bowls and serve hot.

CRAB & GINGER SOUP

(serves 4)

Ingredients

- 1 carrot, chopped.
- 1 leek, chopped.
- 1 bay leaf.
- 900ml/11/2pt fish stock.
- 2 medium cooked crabs.
- 2.5cm/1in piece of fresh root ginger, peeled and grated.
- 1 teaspoon light soy sauce.
- 1/2 teaspoon ground star anise.
- salt and freshly ground black pepper.

Procedure

1. Put the carrot and leek in a large heavy saucepan with the bay leaf and the fish stock. Bring to the boil, reduce the heat, cover and leave to simmer for 10 minutes or until the vegetables are nearly tender.

2. Remove all of the meat from the crabs. Break off and reserve the claws; break the joints and remove the meat using a fork;

3. Add the crabmeat to the pan together with the ginger, soy sauce and star anise, and bring to the boil. Leave to simmer for about 10 minutes until the vegetables are tender and the crab is heated through;

4. Season the soup with salt and pepper, then ladle into warm individual serving bowls and garnish with the crab claws. Serve immediately.

CULLEN SKINK

(serves 4)

Ingredients

- 225g/8oz smoked haddock fillet.
- 25g/1oz butter.
- 1 onion, finely chopped.
- 600ml/1pt milk.
- 350g/12oz potatoes, diced.
- 350g/12oz cod, boned, skinned and cubed.
- 150ml/5fl oz double cream.
- 2 tablespoons chopped fresh flat-leaf parsley.
- salt and freshly ground black pepper.

Procedure

1. Put the haddock fillet in a large frying pan and cover with boiling water. Let stand for 10 minutes, then drain, reserving 300ml/10fl oz of the soaking water. Flake the fish, taking care to remove all the bones;

2. Melt the butter in a large saucepan over a low heat. Add the onion and sweat gently for 10 minutes until softened. Add the milk and bring to a gentle simmer before adding the potatoes. Cook for 10 minutes;

3. Add the reserved haddock flakes and the cod. Simmer for a further 10 minutes until the cod is tender. Remove about one-third of the fish and potatoes, put in a blender or food processor and purée until smooth. Return to the soup with the cream, parsley and salt and pepper to taste. Add a little of the reserved soaking water if the soup seems too thick. Reheat gently and serve hot.

SPICY OATMEAL SOUP

(serves 8)

Ingredients

- 15g/1/2oz margarine.
- 1 tablespoon groundnut oil.
- 2 large leeks, thinly sliced.
- 4 carrots, sliced.
- 2 potatoes, diced.
- 2 celery sticks, sliced.
- 1.2 litres/2pt chicken stock.
- 1 tablespoon dried chives.
- 1 tablespoon dried shallots.
- 1/2 tablespoon dried tarragon.
- 1/2 tablespoon dried basil.

- 1 teaspoon salt.
- 100g/4oz oatmeal.
- 225ml/8fl oz white wine.

Procedure

1. at the margarine and groundnut oil in a large saucepan over a medium-high heat. Add the leeks and sweat for 2-3 minutes;

2. Add the carrots, potatoes, celery and chicken stock. Bring to the boil;

3. Sprinkle in the chives, shallots, tarragon, basil and salt. Boil gently for 20 minutes. Add the oatmeal and cook for a further 5 minutes. Add the wine, cook for 15 minutes more and serve hot.

Book 2:

FRUIT DESSERT
RECIPES FOR
BEGINNERS

Table of contents

GRILLED PINK GRAPEFRUIT

(Serves 4)

Ingredients

- 2 pink grapefruit.
- 1 teaspoon granulated sugar.
- 4 scoops vanilla ice cream.

Procedure

1. Halve the grapefruit and cut round the edge of each, between the pith and the flesh. Separate the segments. Sprinkle each grapefruit with sugar.
2. Put in ramekins to keep them flesh side up, and put on a grill pan. Grill for 2–3 minutes until starting to lightly brown. Put a scoop of vanilla ice cream on top of each, and serve immediately.

LIME SHERBET

(Serves 4)

Ingredients

- 8 limes.
- 75g/3oz caster sugar.
- pinch of salt.
- crushed ice, to serve.

Procedure

1. Squeeze the limes and pour the juice into a large jug. Add the sugar and salt. Stir until dissolved

2. Pour in 1.5 litres/21/2pt water, and top up with plenty of ice to serve.

MANDARINS IN SYRUP

(Serves 4)

Ingredients

- 10 mandarin oranges.
- 15g/1/2oz icing sugar.
- 2 teaspoons orange-flower water.
- 15g/1/2oz chopped pistachio nuts.

Procedure

1. Thinly pare a little of the zest from 1 mandarin, and cut into fine shreds for decoration. Squeeze the juice from 2 mandarins and set aside;

2. Peel the remaining mandarins, removing as much of the white pith as possible. Arrange the peeled fruit whole in a large glass dish;

3. Mix the reserved mandarin juice, sugar and orange-flower water, and pour it over the fruit. Cover the dish and chill for at least an hour;

4. Blanch the shreds of mandarin zest in boiling water for 30 seconds. Drain and leave to cool;

5. To serve, sprinkle the shreds of zest and pistachio nuts over the mandarins, and serve immediately.

FRESH FIGS IN WINE

(Serves 6)

Ingredients

- 450ml/3/4pt dry white wine.
- 75g/3oz clear honey.
- 50g/2oz caster sugar.
- 1 small orange.
- 8 whole cloves.
- 450g/1lb fresh figs.
- 1 cinnamon stick.

Procedure

1. Put the wine, honey and sugar in a heavy saucepan, and heat gently until the sugar dissolves;
2. Stud the orange with the cloves, and add to the syrup with the figs and cinnamon. Cover and simmer until the figs are soft;
3. Transfer to a serving dish, and leave to cool before serving.

ORANGE & DATE SALAD

(Serves 6)

Ingredients

- 6 oranges.
- 2 tablespoons orange-flower water.
- 100g/4oz stoned dates, chopped.
- 50g/2oz pistachio nuts, chopped.
- 15g/1/2oz icing sugar.
- 1 teaspoon toasted almonds.

Procedure

1. Peel the oranges with a sharp knife, removing all the pith. Cut into segments, catching all the juice in a bowl. Put the segments in a serving dish.

2. Stir in the juice from the bowl and the orange-flower water.

3. Sprinkle the dates and nuts over the salad, along with the icing sugar. Chill for 1 hour.

4. Just before serving, sprinkle with the toasted almonds.

CALIFORNIAN BAKED PEARS

(Serves 4)

Ingredients

- 25g/1oz butter.
- 1 teaspoon granulated sugar..
- grated zest of 1/2 lemon.
- 4 dessert pears.
- 300g/11oz canned fruit cocktail in syrup.
- 1/2 teaspoon mixed spice.

Procedure

1. Preheat the oven to 190°C/375°F/Gas mark 5;

2. Melt the butter in a flameproof casserole dish. Add the sugar and lemon zest. Peel the pears, and turn in this mixture. Cover and bake for 30 minutes;

3. Add the fruit cocktail and its syrup, and sprinkle with the mixed spice. Return to the oven for 10 minutes;

4. Lift the pears out onto warmed plates. Stir the fruit cocktail well into the pan juices. Spoon around the pears, and serve immediately.

BANANA SPLIT

(Serves 4)

Ingredients

- 200g/7oz dark chocolate (at least 70% cocoa solids).
- 175ml/6fl oz double cream.
- 25g/1oz butter.
- 4 bananas.
- 12 scoops vanilla ice cream.
- mixed chopped nuts, to serve.

Procedure

1. Put the chocolate, cream and butter in a pan, and stir over a low heat until smooth. Cool slightly;

2. Split the bananas in half lengthways, and arrange in four glass dishes. Put 3 scoops of ice cream in each dish, and pour the chocolate sauce over the top;

3. Sprinkle with the chopped nuts, and serve immediately.

SUMMER BERRIES IN CHAMPAGNE JELLY

(Serves 8)

Ingredients

- 900ml/11/2pt Champagne.
- 11/2 teaspoons powdered gelatine.
- 250g/9oz granulated sugar.
- 250g/9oz strawberries, hulled and chopped.
- 250g/9oz blueberries.

Procedure

1. Pour half of the champagne into a large bowl, and let the bubbles subside. Sprinkle the gelatine over the top in an even layer. Do not stir. Leave until the gelatine is spongy;

2. Pour the remaining Champagne into a large saucepan, add the sugar and heat gently, stirring constantly, until all the sugar has dissolved. Remove the pan from the heat, add the gelatine mixture and stir until thoroughly dissolved. Cool completely;

3. Divide the berries among eight 125ml/4fl oz stemmed wine glasses, and gently pour the jelly over them. Chill in the refrigerator until set. Remove from the refrigerator 15 minutes before serving.

MANGO & MELON GINGER SALAD

(Serves 4)

Ingredients

- 2 avocados, peeled, stoned and flesh cut into slices.
- 1 mango, peeled and cut into slices.
- 1 cantaloupe melon, peeled and cut into slices.
- Grated zest and juice of 2 limes.
- 100g/4oz Stilton cheese, crumbled.
- 2 tablespoons finely chopped stem ginger.
- 2 passion fruit, halved.

Procedure

1. Arrange the slices of avocado, mango and melon decoratively on a serving plate.
2. Sprinkle the fruit with the lime zest and juice, Stilton and ginger. Spoon the passion fruit over the salad and serve.

MUSCAT GRAPE FRAPPÉ

(Serves 4)

Ingredients

- 1/2 bottle Muscat wine.
- 450g/1lb Muscat grapes.

Procedure

1. Pour the wine into a stainless-steel baking tray, add 150ml/5fl oz water and freeze for 3 hours or until completely solid;

2. Scrape the frozen wine with a tablespoon to make a fine ice. Combine the grapes with the ice, and spoon into four shallow glasses. Serve immediately.

SUMMER FRUITS WITH RICOTTA & VANILLA DIP

(Serves 4)

Ingredients

- 250g/9oz ricotta cheese.
- 250g/9oz mascarpone cheese.
- 150ml/5fl oz crème fraiche.
- a few drops of vanilla essence.
- grated zest of 1 lemon.
- 50g/2oz caster sugar.
- 900g/2lb mixed fresh summer berries.

Procedure

- Beat the cheeses together with the crème fraîche, vanilla essence, lemon zest and sugar. Spoon into a serving dish, cover and chill for at least 30 minutes;
- To serve, pile the berries onto a serving plate, and spoon the ricotta and vanilla dip on top.

MULLED FLORIDA COCKTAIL

(Serves 6)

Ingredients

- 2 grapefruit.
- 2 oranges.
- 150ml/5fl oz apple juice.
- 1 tablespoon brandy.
- 2 fresh cherries, pitted and halved.

Procedure

1. Over a saucepan to catch the juice, remove all zest and pith from the grapefruit and oranges, and separate each into segments;

2. Put the segments in the saucepan. Add the apple juice and brandy. Heat through until almost boiling.

3. Spoon into four glass dishes and top each with half a cherry. Serve warm.

ETON MESS

(Serves 4)

Ingredients

- 150ml/5fl oz double cream, lightly whipped.

- 200ml/7fl oz Greek-style yogurt.

- 500g/1lb 2oz strawberries, hulled.

- 2 tablespoons crème de cassis.

- 5 meringue nests.

Procedure

1. Fold the cream into the yogurt and chill for 30 minutes;

2. Put 250g/9oz strawberries in a blender or food processor, blend to a purée, then stir in the crème de cassis. Measure out 75ml/3fl oz of the purée and reserve;

3. Slice the remaining strawberries into a bowl, reserving 6 for decoration, then pour the purée over and chill in the bowl for 20 minutes;

4. Break up the meringue nests, and carefully fold into the cream mixture along with the strawberry mixture. Divide between six serving glasses, then drizzle over the reserved purée;

5. Decorate with the reserved strawberries, and serve.

STRAWBERRIES ROMANOFF

(Serves 4)

Ingredients

- 750g/1lb 11oz strawberries, quartered.
- 2 tablespoons Cointreau.
- 1/2 teaspoon finely grated.
- orange zest.
- 15g/1/2oz caster sugar.
- 125ml/4fl oz double cream.
- 20g/3/4oz icing sugar.

Procedure

1. Combine the strawberries, Cointreau, orange zest and caster sugar in a large bowl, cover and refrigerate for 1 hour. Drain the strawberries, reserving any juices;

2. Purée about a quarter of the strawberries with the reserved juices in a blender or food processor. Divide the remaining strawberries among four glasses;

3. Beat the cream and icing sugar until soft peaks form, then fold the strawberry purée through the whipped cream. Spoon the mixture over the top of the strawberries, cover and refrigerate until needed.

SUMMER FRUITS WITH RICOTTA & VANILLA DIP

(Serves 6)

Ingredients

- 250g/9oz ricotta cheese.
- 250g/9oz mascarpone cheese.
- 150ml/5fl oz crème fraiche.
- a few drops of vanilla essence.
- grated zest of 1 lemon.
- 50g/2oz caster sugar.
- 900g/2lb mixed fresh summer berries.

Procedure

1. Beat the cheeses together with the crème fraîche, vanilla essence, lemon zest and sugar. Spoon into a serving dish, cover and chill for at least 30 minutes;
2. To serve, pile the berries onto a serving plate, and spoon the ricotta and vanilla dip on top.

STRAWBERRIES ROMANOFF

(Serves 4)

Ingredients

- 750g/1lb 11oz strawberries, quartered.
- 2 tablespoons Cointreau.
- 1/2 teaspoon finely grated.
- orange zest.
- 15g/1/2oz caster sugar.
- 125ml/4fl oz double cream.
- 20g/3/4oz icing sugar.

Procedure

1. Combine the strawberries, Cointreau, orange zest and caster sugar in a large bowl, cover and refrigerate for 1 hour. Drain the strawberries, reserving any juices;
2. Purée about a quarter of the strawberries with the reserved juices in a blender or food processor. Divide the remaining strawberries among four glasses;
3. Beat the cream and icing sugar until soft peaks form, then fold the strawberry purée through the whipped cream. Spoon the mixture over the top of the strawberries, cover and refrigerate until needed.

BANANAS WITH CHOCOLATE MARSHMALLOW SAUCE

(Serves 4)

Ingredients

- 4 slightly unripe bananas.
- 50g/2oz chocolate chips.
- 24 mini marshmallows.

Procedure

1. Preheat the oven to 160°C/325°F/Gas mark 3.

2. Trim the ends of the bananas, leaving on the skins. Using a sharp knife, make a lengthways slit in each one;

3. Gently prise open each banana, and fill with chocolate chips and marshmallows, then wrap each banana in foil. Bake in the oven for 15–20 minutes, and serve hot.

PINEAPPLE FLAMBÉ

(Serves 4)

Ingredients

- 1 large ripe pineapple, about 600g/1 1/4lb.
- 25g/1oz butter.
- 50g/2oz soft brown sugar.
- 50ml/2fl oz freshly squeezed orange juice.
- 25ml/1fl oz vodka.
- 1 tablespoon slivered almonds, toasted.

Procedure

- Cut away the top and base of the pineapple, then cut down the sides, removingNall the dark 'eyes'. Cut the pineapple into thin slices. Using an apple corer, remove the hard, central core from each slice;

- Melt the butter in a frying pan with the sugar. Add the orange juice and stir until hot. Add as many pineapple slices as the pan will hold, and cook for 1-2 minutes, turning once. As each pineapple slice browns, remove to a plate;

- Return all the pineapple slices to the pan, heat briefly, then pour over the vodka and carefully light with a long match. Let the flames die down, then sprinkle with the almonds and serve at once.

SPICED FRUIT PLATTER

(Serves 6)

Ingredients

- 1 pineapple
- 2 papayas
- 1 small cantaloupe melon
- juice of 2 limes
- 2 pomegranates
- chat masala, to taste

Procedure

1. Cut away the top and base of the pineapple, then cut down the sides, removing all the dark 'eyes'. Cut the pineapple into thin slices. Using an apple corer, remove the hard, central core from each slice;

2. Peel the papayas. Cut them in half, then into thin wedges. Halve the melon and remove the seeds from the middle. Cut into thin wedges and remove the skin;

3. Arrange the fruit on six individual plates, and sprinkle with the lime juice. Cut the pomegranates in half, and scoop out the seeds, discarding any bitter pith. Scatter the seeds over the fruit;

4. Serve, sprinkled with a little chat masala to taste.

GRILLED FRESH FIGS WITH CRÉME FRAÎCHE

(Serves 4)

Ingredients

- 8 ripe fresh figs.
- 225g/8oz créme fraiche.
- 50g/2oz light muscovado sugar.

Procedure

1. Preheat the grill to high. Lightly butter a shallow flameproof dish, large enough to accommodate the figs in a single layer.

2. Cut the figs into quarters without cutting through the base, and gently open each one out a little. Spoon a dollop of crème fraîche into the centre of each fig.

3. Sprinkle the sugar evenly between the figs. Put the figs in the prepared dish, and put the hot grill for 2 minutes or until the sugar has melted and the crème fraîche starts to run. Serve immediately.

POACHED ALLSPICE PEARS

(Serves 4)

Ingredients

- 4 large dessert pears, peeled, cored and halved.
- 300ml/10fl oz orange juice.
- 2 teaspoons ground allspice.
- 50g/2oz raisins.
- 25g/1oz Demerara sugar.

Procedure

1. Put the pears in a large saucepan. Add the orange juice, ground allspice, raisins and sugar, and heat gently, stirring, until the sugar has dissolved. Bring the mixture to the boil and continue to boil for 1 minute.

2. Reduce the heat to low, and leave to simmer for about 10 minutes. Test to see if the pears are soft and cooked by inserting the tip of a sharp knife. When they are ready, remove the pears from the pan with a slotted spoon and transfer to serving plates.

3. Serve hot with the syrup.

GRILLED FRESH FIGS WITH CRÉME FRAÎCHE

(Serves 4)

Ingredients

- 8 ripe fresh figs.
- 225g/8oz créme fraiche.
- 50g/2oz light muscovado sugar.

Procedure

1. Preheat the grill to high. Lightly butter a shallow flameproof dish, large enough to accommodate the figs in a single layer;
2. Cut the figs into quarters without cutting through the base, and gently open each one out a little. Spoon a dollop of crème fraîche into the centre of each fig;
3. Sprinkle the sugar evenly between the figs. Put the figs in the prepared dish, and put the hot grill for 2 minutes or until the sugar has melted and the crème fraîche starts to run. Serve immediately.

MELON AND ORANGE CUPS

(Serves 4)

Ingredients

- 2 small honeydew melons.
- 1 grapefruit, peeled and segmented.
- 2 oranges, peeled and segmented.
- 50g/2oz roasted, unsalted peanuts.
- 25g/1oz light muscovado sugar.
- 1/4 teaspoon ground cinnamon.

Procedure

1. Halve the melons, scoop out the seeds and discard, then remove and chop the flesh. Reserve the melon shells;
2. In a bowl, mix together the melon and citrus fruits. Pile the fruits back into the melon shells;
3. Chop the peanuts and mix with the sugar and cinnamon. Sprinkle over the fruit and serve.

MELON MEDLEY

(Serves 4)

Ingredients

- 1/2 cantaloupe melon.
- 1/2 honeydew melon.
- 1/2 watermelon.
- pulp from 2 passion fruit.

Procedure

1. Cut the melons into bite-size pieces, or use a melon baller to slice into balls. Chill, covered, for 30 minutes;
2. Drizzle with the passion fruit pulp before serving.

PINEAPPLE & PASSION FRUIT SALSA

(Serves 6)

Ingredients

- 1 small pineapple.
- 2 passion fruit.
- 150ml/5fl oz Greek-style yogurt.
- 2 tablespoons light muscovado sugar.

Procedure

1. Cut the top and bottom of the pineapple. Using a large sharp knife, slice off the peel and remove any remaining 'eyes'. Slice the pineapple, and use a small pastry cutter or an apple corer to remove the tough core from each slice;

2. Cut the passion fruit in half, and scoop the seeds and pulp into a bowl. Stir in the pineapple slices and yogurt. Cover and chill;

3. Stir in the sugar just before serving.

SNOW-CAPPED APPLES

(Serves 4)

Ingredients

- 4 small cooking apples.
- 75ml/3fl oz orange marmalade.
- 2 egg whites.
- 50g/2oz caster sugar.

Procedure

1. Preheat the oven to 180°C/350°F/Gas mark 4.

2. Core the apples and score through the skins around the middle with a sharp knife.

3. Put the apples in a wide ovenproof dish, and spoon 1 tablespoon marmalade into the centre of each. Cover and bake in the oven for 35–40 minutes until tender.

4. Whisk the egg whites in a large bowl until stiff enough to hold soft peaks. Whisk in the sugar, then fold in the remaining marmalade.

5. Spoon the meringue over the apples, then return to the oven for 10–15 minutes. Serve immediately.

RED FRUIT SALAD

(Serves 4)

Ingredients

- 250g/9oz strawberries, hulled and halved
- 100g/4oz raspberries
- 250g/9oz cherries, pitted
- 1 tablespoon Cointreau
- 1 tablespoon soft brown sugar

Procedure

1. Put the strawberries, raspberries and cherries in a bowl, drizzle with Cointreau, cover and set aside for 20 minutes;
2. Put the sugar and 2 tablespoons water in a small pan. Stir over a gentle heat for 3 minutes or until the sugar has dissolved. Cool, pour over the fruit, and serve.

GRILLED APPLE STACK

(Serves 4)

Ingredients

- 4 large dessert apples, cored and peeled
- 25g/1oz butter
- 1 × 400g/14oz jar lime marmalade
- 4 scoops vanilla ice cream

Procedure

1. Cut the apples into thin slices across the core, and put on a lightly greased grill tray. Top each slice with a small piece of butter and 1/2 teaspoon lime marmalade;

2. Cook under a hot grill until the butter has melted and the apple is golden brown;

3. Serve 4 or 5 slices stacked on top of each other, with a scoop of vanilla ice cream alongside.

GRAPEFRUIT IN APRICOT BRANDY

(Serves 4)

Ingredients

- 3 grapefruit.
- 125ml/4fl oz apple juice.
- 11/2 teaspoons granulated sugar.
- 2.5cm/1in piece of cinnamon stick.
- 3 tablespoons apricot brandy.
- 3 ready-to-eat dried apricots, chopped.

Procedure

1. Cut off all the zest and pith from the grapefruit, working over a shallow pan to catch any juice. Push out the white core using the handle of a teaspoon, then thickly slice the grapefruit;

2. Put the apple juice and sugar in the pan with the cinnamon stick. Bring to the boil, and simmer for 3 minutes. Add the fruit and simmer for 6–8 minutes;

3. Remove the fruit from the pan and transfer to four warmed serving plates. Add the apricot brandy to the juice. Bring back to the boil, then spoon over the fruit and sprinkle with the chopped apricots. Serve immediately.

BLUSHING PEARS

(Serves 6)

Ingredients

- 6 dessert pears.
- 300ml/10fl oz rosé wine.
- 150ml/5fl oz cranberry juice.
- strip of thinly pared orange zest.
- 1 cinnamon stick.
- 4 whole cloves.
- 1 bay leaf.
- 75g/3oz caster sugar.

Procedure

1. Thinly peel the pears with a sharp knife or vegetable peeler, leaving the stalks intact.

2. Pour the wine and cranberry juice into a large heavy pan. Add the orange zest, cinnamon stick, cloves, bay leaf and sugar. Heat gently, stirring all the time, until the sugar has dissolved. Add the pears, standing them upright in the pan. Pour in enough cold water to barely cover them.

3. Cover and cook gently for 20–30 minutes until just tender, turning and basting with the syrup occasionally. Using a slotted spoon, gently lift the pears out of the syrup and transfer to a serving dish.

4. Bring the syrup to the boil, and boil rapidly for 10–15 minutes until it has reduced by half. Strain the syrup and pour over the pears. Serve.

SWEET-STEWED DRIED FRUIT

(Serves 4)

Ingredients

- 500g/1lb 2oz mixed dried fruit salad.
- 450ml/3/pt apple juice.
- 2 tablespoons clear honey.
- 2 tablespoons brandy.
- grated zest and juice of 1 lemon.
- grated zest and juice of 1 orange.

Procedure

1. Put the fruit salad, apple juice, honey, brandy, lemon and orange zests and juices in a small saucepan. Bring to the boil, and simmer for about 1 minute;
2. Remove the pan from the heat, and allow the mixture to cool completely. Transfer to a large bowl, cover with cling film and chill in the refrigerator overnight;
3. To serve, spoon the stewed fruit into four shallow dishes.

GRAPEFRUIT IN APRICOT BRANDY

(Serves 4)

Ingredients

- 3 grapefruit.
- 125ml/4fl oz apple juice.
- 11/2 teaspoons granulated sugar.
- 2.5cm/1in piece of cinnamon stick.
- 3 tablespoons apricot brandy.
- 3 ready-to-eat dried apricots, chopped.

Procedure

1. Cut off all the zest and pith from the grapefruit, working over a shallow pan to catch any juice. Push out the white core using the handle of a teaspoon, then thickly slice the grapefruit;

2. Put the apple juice and sugar in the pan with the cinnamon stick. Bring to the boil, and simmer for 3 minutes. Add the fruit and simmer for 6–8 minutes;

3. Remove the fruit from the pan and transfer to four warmed serving plates. Add the apricot brandy to the juice. Bring back to the boil, then spoon over the fruit and sprinkle with the chopped apricots. Serve immediately.

PEACH MELBA

(Serves 4)

Ingredients

- 300g/11oz fresh raspberries.
- 25g/1oz icing sugar.
- 375g/13oz granulated sugar.
- 1 vanilla pod, split lengthways.
- 4 peaches.
- 4 scoops vanilla ice cream.

Procedure

1. Purée the raspberries and icing sugar together in a blender or food processor. Pass through a sieve and discard the seeds;

2. Stir the sugar, vanilla pod and 600ml/1pt water in a pan over a low heat until the sugar has completely dissolved;

3. Bring the sugar syrup to the boil, and add the peaches, ensuring that they are covered with the syrup. Simmer for 5 minutes or until tender, then remove the peaches with a slotted spoon and carefully remove the skin;

4. To serve, put a scoop of ice cream on each plate, add a peach and spoon raspberry purée on top.

STRAWBERRIES IN GRAPE JELLY

(Serves 4)

Ingredients

- 500ml/18fl oz red grape juice.
- 1 cinnamon stick.
- pared zest and juice of 1 small orange.
- 1 tablespoon powdered gelatine.
- 225g/8oz strawberries, hulled and chopped.

Procedure

1. Pour the grape juice into a pan, and add the cinnamon stick and orange zest. Cook over a very low heat for 10 minutes, then strain the juice and discard the flavourings;
2. Sprinkle the powdered gelatine over the orange juice in a small bowl. When the mixture is spongy, stir into the grape juice until it has completely dissolved.
3. Allow the jelly to cool in the bowl until just beginning to set. Stir in the strawberries, and pour into a 900ml/11/2pt mould. Chill until set.

PERSIAN MELON CUPS

(Serves 4)

Ingredients

- 2 small cantaloupe melons.
- 225g/8oz strawberries, hulled and sliced.
- 3 peaches, peeled and cubed.
- 225g/8oz seedless white grapes.
- 25g/1oz caster sugar.
- 1 tablespoon rose water.
- 1 tablespoon freshly squeezed lemon juice.
- crushed ice, to serve.

Procedure

1. Carefully cut the melons in half and remove the seeds. Scoop out the flesh with a melon baller, taking care not to damage the skin. Reserve the melon shells.
2. Put the strawberries in a large mixing bowl with the melon balls, peaches, grapes, sugar, rose water and lemon juice;
3. •Pile the fruit into the melon shells, and chill in the refrigerator for 2 hours;
4. To serve, sprinkle with the crushed ice, and serve immediately.

NECTARINES WITH MARZIPAN & YOGURT

(Serves 4)

Ingredients

- Nectarines.
- 75g/3oz marzipan.
- 75ml/3fl oz Greek-style yogurt.
- 3 amaretti biscuits, crushed.

Procedure

1. Cut the nectarines in half, removing the stones. Cut the marzipan into 8 pieces, and press one piece into the stone cavity of each nectarine half. Preheat the grill.

2. Spoon the Greek yogurt on top of the nectarines. Sprinkle the crushed amaretti biscuits over the yogurt. Put the fruits under the grill for 3-5 minutes until the yogurt starts to melt. Serve immediately.

GOOSEBERRY CHEESE COOLER

(Serves 4)

Ingredients

- 500g/1lb 2oz fresh gooseberries.
- finely grated zest and juice of 1 small orange.
- 1 tablespoon clear honey.
- 250g/9oz cottage cheese.

Procedure

1. Top and tail the gooseberries, and put them in a pan. Add the orange zest and juice, and cook gently, stirring occasionally, until the fruit is tender. Remove from the heat and stir in the honey.

2. Purée the gooseberries and their juice in a blender or food processor until almost smooth. Allow to cool.

3. Press the cottage cheese through a sieve until smooth. Stir half of the cooled gooseberry purée into the cottage cheese.

4. To serve, spoon the cheese mixture into four serving glasses. Top each one with gooseberry purée, and serve chilled.

POACHED PEACHES WITH GINGER

(Serves 4)

Ingredients

- 4 peaches, halved and stoned.
- 125ml/4fl oz water.
- 2 tablespoons lemon juice 1cm/1/2 in root ginger, peeled and grated 1 cinnamon.
- Stick.
- 225g/8oz seedless white grapes, halved.

Procedure

1. Preheat the oven to 180°C/350°F/Gas mark 4.

2. Put the peach halves skin side up in a baking dish.;Combine 125ml/4fl oz water, the lemon juice, ginger and cinnamon stick, and pour over the peaches. Poach in the oven for 30 minutes;

3. Remove from the oven and arrange the peaches on four dessert plates. Top with the cooking juices, add the grapes and serve immediately.

FRUIT FONDUE

(Serves 2)

Ingredients

- 50g/2oz soft cheese.
- 150ml/5fl oz hazelnut yogurt.
- 1 teaspoon vanilla essence.
- 1 teaspoon caster sugar.
- selection of fresh fruits for dipping, such as strawberries, satsumas, kiwi fruit, grapes, all cut into bite-size pieces • Beat the soft cheese with the yogurt, vanilla essence and sugar in a bowl.

Procedure

1. Spoon the mixture into a glass serving dish set on a platter. Arrange the prepared fruits around the dip, and serve immediately.

LIME SHERBET

(Serves 6)

Ingredients

- Limes.
- 75g/3oz caster sugar.
- pinch of salt.
- crushed ice, to serve.

Procedure

2. Squeeze the limes and pour the juice into a large jug. Add the sugar and salt. Stir until dissolved • Pour in 1.5 litres/21/2pt water, and top up with plenty of ice to serve.

GRILLED PINK GRAPEFRUIT

(Serves 4)

Ingredients

- 2 pink grapefruit.
- 1 teaspoon granulated sugar.
- 4 scoops vanilla ice cream.

Procedure

3. Halve the grapefruit and cut round the edge of each, between the pith and the flesh. Separate the segments. Sprinkle each grapefruit with sugar.

4. Put in ramekins to keep them flesh side up, and put on a grill pan. Grill for 2–3 minutes until starting to lightly brown. Put a scoop of vanilla ice cream on top of each, and serve immediately.

Thank you for purchasing this recipe book!

If you want to learn more delicious recipes, check the other titles of this series.

Michelle Desire

CPSIA information can be obtained
at www.ICGtesting.com
Printed in the USA
BVHW062011140521
607271BV00007B/634